AF612379

mortal

love, self, & everything else

by carter zane

dedications

this book is dedicated to my eight year old self,
who never believed that he would come out, find happiness,
or experience the love that he craved.

this book is also dedicated to each and every queer person,
especially young queer people.
your life matters,
your love is beautiful,
your dreams are obtainable.
i promise to fight for you…
always.

acknowledgments

i have many people to thank
for their help in creating this piece of art.
thank you:
to erin ouellette, my chief editor and mother.
to anya ouellette, my best friend and loudest cheerleader.
to saskia lynge, a contributor, friend, and mentor.
to berlin roberts, my trusted ally and close friend.
to camille anderson, who contributed much encouragement.

foreword

Some books are written as a labor of love,
as a form of expression, and as a creative outlet.
My firm belief is that Carter, my oldest son,
wrote this anthology out of necessity.
He wrote the poems contained herein to process and release
the pain, the heartache, the confusion…
the raw emotions he kept inside for so long.
As a first hand witness to his life,
I desire to share with each reader
just how honest his writings are…
how true are his struggles…
how real is his pain…
how hopeful is his future.
He no longer lives in the shadows of fear and doubt,
though it still tries to creep in.
Be encouraged, reader.
Carter is moving forward in life.
Growing, healing, and learning with each step he takes.
So can you.
Hear his past but know that he no longer lives there.
Feel his wounds but be assured that he is still fighting.
For himself.
And for others like him.
Carter, I am proud to call you my son.

- *Erin Ouellette*

while my hope for this collection of poetry
is peace, understanding, and growth,
i also want to make it clear
that this poetry may not be suitable for all readers.
while i tackle intense issues in a soft manner,
mentions of sexual abuse,
emotional abuse,
and self-harm
are still included in these pages.
the experiences i have written about are my own,
but they may disturb some readers.

trigger warning:

self-harm

mental illness

sexual abuse

parental abuse

religious trauma

childhood trauma

mortal

love, self, & everything else

summary of contents:

part one: *love & heartbreak………… 17*

within *part one*, you will find anger, forgiveness,
love, and more anger. not so much angry with someone,
more so *angry with love*. furious, even.

part two: *family, self, & others………… 187*

within *part two*, you will find utter fury.
but, even in the midst of the fury, i hope you see the growth.
i hope you see the acceptance of the way things are.
part two, while shorter in length, carries more weight.
i poured my heart into the poems contained in part two.
revisiting trauma, abuse, and emotional wounds is no easy task.
many poems will surely upset some individuals,
but i speak from the heart and do so honestly.
furthermore, poetry is a place to let anger,
chaos, jealousy, envy, and strife run *completely unhindered.*

dear reader,

you hold many secrets in your hand.
treat them well.
read them carefully.

with love,

c.z.

part one:

love & heartbreak

kisses in quicksand

you asked to kiss me
and i said *yes*
we ended up dancing
now you want me less
you said that you get me
so i gave you a key
the key to my heart
you held in your hand
but your love ended up
being quicksand

ropes

my heart said to hope
but you had me wrapped in rope
little did i know
that rope was a noose
i just never thought
you would cut me loose

stargazing alone

i look up at the stars
and i wonder where you are
do you feel the same breeze that i do
do you hear the same sounds that i do
do you feel the same pain that i do
are you thinking of me
as i am thinking of you

cuts from the calendar

in just ten short days
i gave you my heart
and with one simple word
you tore it apart

growing apart

i wanted to grow old with you
not grow apart from you

loneliness
the deepest abyss
you fall and hope someone will catch you
only to find out that no one will
the people who pushed you into the abyss
do not even regret
do not even miss
they've already found someone else to kiss

nobody like you

everyone is *replaceable*
but i don't think i am capable
my feelings for you are not just occasional
or even debatable
they are not fragile or breakable
because you are *irreplaceable*

lying to myself

my attempted refutation
of my deep infatuation
only hurt my reputation
i know i still want you
so why should i lie
or hide
or deny
i think you still want me
at least that is what you said
but you let fear get into your head

purple bookshops

at the bookshop
you looked at me
and said *stop*
you leaned in
kissed my cheek
and i was put together again

abusive artist

in the beginning
you painted my sky golden
halfway through
that sky became blue
in the end
my sky was black
and bloody
and bruised
your changing colors
left me confused
once again
i have fallen for a trap
and ended up abused

goodbye

your voice echos in my mind
your words have me entwined
your voice is smooth
and sweet
and gentle
your words are never judgmental
sadly
your voice is not mine to hear
sadly
your voice is no longer here
it left me when you said *goodbye*
with that word
you let us die
now that you are gone
all i can do is cry

my type

his hair was soft
his hands were rough
his eyes were brown
his skin was smooth
i can still see him
sitting across from me

january 8, 2021

i felt your body underneath mine
i kissed your lips
i touched your face
i ran my fingers through your hair
as we sat outside
with the cold winter air
but you never told me to prepare
or that i would need someone else to repair
repair all that you left with me with
which is nothing but despair

oriental garden

you drove us to that restaurant
the mood was everything but nonchalant
i heard your nervous breath
saw your tense body
caught a glimpse of your anxious eyes
you and i sat face to face
the three feet between us
felt like so much space
too much space
i really don't enjoy that space
i only want your enchanting embrace

last summer

we swayed together under streetlight
you had me convinced that our future was bright
but i should have been more alert that night
because you chose flight instead of fight

goodbye is just a word
but in the end
it was the word that took you
away from me

june 2

i know your favorite color
it's purple-ish blue
i know that you love to try new things
even the things you know you can't do
i know about your pain
and that you prefer sunshine to rain
you love a good book
a good movie
a good song
i know that for love
you have waited so very long
i know you well enough to know
where you belong
you belong next to me
i think you and i should become a *we*

nightowl

our phone calls lasted for hours
they were water for my wilting flowers
hearing your voice made me giddy inside
then you pulled away
and my flowers suddenly died

february

you are on trial for breaking my heart
my testimony will rip you apart
because i remember all the pain
of your reckless game
and now you are here
so i will ruin your name

the last *goodbye*
cut deeper than a knife
i thought you were
the love of my life
now all that is left
is deep seated strife

a sophist at heart

it is hard to find a silver lining
when, for you,
i am still pining
even after all your lying

a boy with a girl

green-light
red-light
gaslight
wasn’t ready for this fight
green-light
red-light
gaslight
the signs sat in plain sight
green-light
red-light
gaslight
walked right into your plight
green-light
red-light
gaslight
you left me in the middle of the night
green-light
red-light
gaslight
my friends were right

my mind is a palace
his love is the king
i am ready to offer him
each and every thing

regret

i miss him so much that my body aches
i made such a painful mistake
i spend so many nights awake
i cannot sleep
because it is him
that i cannot keep

do you not remember when we danced
in that empty parking lot
do you not remember when we kissed
and did not want to stop
do you not remember when you looked at me
and your gaze did not drop
i remember
i still feel it
you just couldn't commit

my heart is a minefield
so much pain is concealed
but you saw the pain
so you came
and you healed

my broken heart made me write it
don't be angry with me
be angry with it
my broken heart made me do it
don't be sad with me
be upset with it
my broken heart made me say it
don't be mad at me
please
just come back to it
my broken heart still longs for you
my broken heart is still in two
my broken heart needs you to mend
please
don't let this be our end

different nightmares

you visit my dreams
everything is never how it seems
you comfort me through all of my aching screams
you pull me out of these deep dark streams

fear was the word of the hour
such a small word
it holds so much power

paramour
i want you more
paramour
teach me your lore
paramour
with you
i soar

i stood here
ready and willing
open and free
why did you turn and flee

parked

i sat in your truck
gazed into your eyes
and realized all my luck
you held me tight
your lips felt so right
but you were gone
before morning light

i was a game to you

i look back and wonder
why are you gone
then realize
i fell for your con
shame on me
i was your willing pawn

olivia rodrigo

you kissed me
while we listened to song about heartbreak
i should have seen the impending ache

accutane

his lips were dry and coarse
but i didn’t mind
because they were his lips
and that was all that mattered to me

and now i know
how those trees feel in winter
frail and bare
and knocked off center
just as bitter wind steals the leaves of the tree
so, too, did your fears take you from me

vindictive

heartbreak
heartbreak
why'd you let my heart break
heartbreak
heartbreak
drowned me in your dark lake
heartbreak
heartbreak
you are so fucking fake
heartbreak
heartbreak
can't wait till you break

somehow
despite doing nothing wrong
i always end up alone
somehow
despite giving it my all
i never give enough
somehow
despite being a stronghold
a safe house
a fighter for love
i never receive the affection i desire

curiosity

what could i have said
to keep you here with me
what should i done
how should i have kissed you
held you
touched you
why did you run
was it something i said
or something i failed to say
what was standing in our way
if only i could go back in time
i would rewrite our story
i would say the right thing
kiss you the right way
and maybe
just maybe
i could have you for one more day

maybe if i could see your past
or meet the one you loved last
i could understand why you left me so fast

a time machine would be useful
right about now
i would not go back and change anything
i would just go back
and tell myself to enjoy you
while i still have you
i would just go back
and simply look at you longer
and hold you tighter

i enjoy the chaos

this *chaotic infatuation*
is the root of my frustration
this *chaotic infatuation*
is the reason for my emotional detonation

denton square

your truck haunts the streets
of *my* city's square
your face is painted on the walls
of *my* favorite bookshop
your voice echoes
throughout that restaurant
you are gone
and yet
you consume everything
that i once called *mine*

not a day goes by
that i do not think of you
i just do not know
what i am supposed to do
not having you is killing me
i will never get to say *we*
you and i were not meant to be

i wake
put clothes on
move through my day
and pretend that i am not thinking of you

gone too soon

i never had the chance to see our movie
you left before it started
i only saw our preview
but just know
that if you had stayed
i would have purchased a ticket

you are gone
never to be kissed again
but i still feel your lips
pressed to mine

a regular stephen king

you authored this book of my pain
why are you mad
when i read it to others

your cover and title led me to believe
that your chapters were full of romance
but
after reading each page
i see that you are a horror novel
and i regret reading you
because now i cannot sleep
without seeing the terror
when i close my eyes

this is the end
i am letting you go
keeping you in my mind
only prolongs my pain
keeping you in my thoughts
only harms my heart
thinking of you
always
keeps me from moving on
so now
i must do the last thing
that i wish to do
say *goodbye*

you feel unique

i am trying to numb myself
to the pain of losing you
with books
and games
and movies
and songs
and friends
but nothing in this world
makes me feel like you do

but
i choose to be unaware
and not to care
i choose to ignore
and not engage in this war
i choose to walk away
and not to stay
i choose to put me first
because for my heart
you are the worst

how is it
that i fell for you
when you were never mine
how is it
that i am still falling for you
even though you are his
these are the questions
that keep me awake
these are the questions
that drive me insane
these are the questions
that haunt my mind
you are the one
that i will never get to kiss
you are the love
i have to learn to miss
you are not mine to love
and how that is
i will never know

when i met you
the flame of your affection
lit my path
now that you are gone
the flame is burning me
and i am dying in the furnace

i am inexorably infatuated
with the thought of you

my body is not a chew toy
for some boy
it is a mother fucking temple
and i expect to be worshiped

same planet

just knowing that you and i
sleep under the same moon
brings me comfort

eternal thunderstorm

hearing your name
brings so much regret
sadness
and pain
losing you was like losing sunshine
and i am forever stuck in the rain

jungle gym

you treated my body like a playground
you skipped around
and when you got bored
you moved on to the next playground

i wish you had a table of contents
i wish i could have seen how the story ended
your first chapter had so much potential
i never saw the plot twist coming

texas boys

preemptively
i should have struck
you clearly didn't give a fuck
i should have never sat in your truck
i wish you all the worst of luck

i used to surf on the waves your tide drew in
now i am drowning in them

there is not enough paper in the world
for me to write out all the ways you hurt me

when i think of you
it will only be when i am remembering
that you are not here
that i do not have you
that you are somewhere else
that you are with someone else

for now
i will continue to pretend
pretend that i do not miss you
pretend that i do not stare at pictures of you
pretend that i do not obsess over a future
that is not
and will never be
because the pain of forgetting you
hurts more
than the pain of my pretending

thinking of you
and how you are not mine
stings
but the thought of forgetting you
stings
stabs
and slits
more aggressively
i will take pain when thinking of you
over not thinking of you ever

even now
after all i know
it is him
i still seek

our first chapter was our last
you are too scarred by your past
for anything more than something
that ends fast

2nd choice

to be young and in love
oh how that must be
but i sit here alone
because he didn’t want me

i wonder if
before you die
you will look back at what we had
and regret not keeping what we were

who did this to you

who taught you to fear love
to never accept it
who taught you to fear another's body
to never touch it
who taught you to fear intimacy
to never engage in it
tell me who it was
i will find them
i will end them

how am i to recover
when i never said goodbye
how was i supposed to know that
that goodbye
was our last

my only worry now
is that i will never find love
because you still hold my heart

how much time i wasted
missing you
when you had your tongue
down another boy’s throat

alone with my mind

i do not know why you left
you left me here to decide
and my mind will decide
all the negative things
i was not pretty enough
i was not talented enough
i was not smart enough
why did you leave me
with these thoughts

i love you
was your best lie
you had me convinced

nothing is the same

driving empty streets without you
walking in the dark without you
listening to music without you
watching movies without you
just is not the same

facetimes
phone calls
texts
all covered in
beautiful lies
that
in hindsight
are ugly

let the question no longer be
why does he not want me
and let it now be
what the fuck is wrong with him

familiar feeling

how unoriginal this heartbreak feels
i have felt this same pain before
it is all i have ever felt
he will tell me he wants me
then he will find a reason to leave
i have grown used to abandonment

it was the idea of *commitment* that you liked
not the action of it
it was the idea of *us* that you liked
not the action of it

stay gone

one time date
that your deep fears ate
you may come back
but it will be too late

did you enjoy
using me like a toy
like something from a store
that you can throw on the floor
when you feel a sense of bore

i have been in love with you
for three long years
from the moment i saw you
i just knew
knew you would make me smile
knew you would make me laugh
knew you would make me happy
this is the life i wanted with you
but you prefer me as friend
so i will now hear
of how you make him smile
of how you make him laugh
of how you make him happy
this is the life he has with you
and i will be here
when you marry your love
still wishing you knew
in my mind
i am saying
i love you and i do
and still saying
i will always be here for you

you love ice cream
boys
music
car rides
kissing
but above all
you love
you

one month
without a word from you
thirty days
without seeing your face
seven hundred twenty hours
without hearing your voice
forty three thousand two hundred minutes
of agony
without you

you were an uninvited guest
but i let you stay
because you led me to believe
that you were kind
that you could love
that you should stay
but that was all a lie
and i regret letting you inside
i should have told you to leave
i should have *never* opened the door

cheap

your love is a knockoff
of something real
but it is still something
that i wish to feel

it is possible
to fall in love with someone
you just met
it is possible
to fall in love with someone
you hardly know
i should know
i have loved you
since day one

normalize
love at first sight
if our hearts capable
of hating someone
we have never known
surely we can fall in love
with someone we have just seen

nights with you
were medicine
for my *romantically sick* heart
you eased the symptoms
and reminded me that
i am capable of loving again
and that i am worthy of all the love

the song you played
when we kissed
is heard in my mind
when i kiss someone else
they hold my hand
but you hold my heart

still on my shoulders
i feel the jacket
you brought to keep me warm
still on my waist
i feel your hands
like when we danced
still on my mind
is the way i felt
when you said
i get you, too

the *chapter of us*
was never complete
it was left on a cliffhanger
never to be read through
never to be passed down
never to be lived
the *chapter of us*
was over
before it even began
our story will
forever be
incomplete

my blank canvas
was painted by you
the sketches
colors
and shapes remain
but you
the painter
are nowhere to be found
you left me half finished
now someone else
can only be given
half of my canvas

you came aboard my ship
and i let you steer *us*
through the night
then you abandoned ship
when the tides became rough

leading man
you played the role well
every *i love you*
sounded so real
every *i miss you*
sounded so genuine
every *i want you*
sounded so believable
what a convincing script you wrote

my obsession with you
led to depression without you
my intuition told me *not* to trust you
but my infatuation won out
my subscription to your love
led to the downfall of my cognition
this state of heartbreak
feels like a mental condition

you are not romeo
you are pinocchio
lies are not love
deceit is not love
secrets are not love
your nose may not grow
but my loathing of you does

overthinking

i am an emotional hoarder
i shove down
suppress
conceal
and cower
i fear what he will think
if he sees my mess
i do not know
what he will say
after seeing all that is piled
every room of my heart
is filled wall to ceiling
with pain
anxiety
heartbreak
and trauma

overthinking *(continued)*

will he want me
in spite of this
will he love me
regardless of everything
will he kiss me
even in the midst of my messy mind
will he give up on me
if i show him everything i hide
every morsel of pain
every drop of anxiety
every scrap of depression
every souvenir of heartbreak
will he choose to remain
or will the extent of my condition
push him away
will the mess i try to hide
force this love
and all future loves
to end

posed as the hero
performed as the villain

pretended you would save me
plagued me with pain

i like you too much
what a line
sounds more like a lie
to mask your fear of love
i like you too much
is a lousy excuse
is a lousy way of saying
i led you on
then changed my mind
from this moment forward
i will seek men who like me
just enough

my friends tell me
you deserve better
but i do not want *better*
i want you

i’m alone in this house
when you left
only i remained
the fire still burns
the music is still playing
the food is still warm
i am keeping this house
exactly the same
just in case
you choose to return

heartbreak showers
bring
love flowers

you leaving
was once my greatest fear
but in hindsight
i see the pain you caused
and my only fear now
is that you will return

your hand
on my thigh
the feeling
in my mind
body shaking
unaware
of what was
to come next
parked your car
in the city square
talked for hours
kissed forever
drove me home
one last kiss
cannot wait for
the next time
you have
your hand
on my thigh

is he coming back
i ask my heart
he is not
and that is a good thing
it responds

the new year
brought you
into my life
as if the universe
heard my call for love
and sent you to love me
as if mother nature
saw my wilting roses
and sent you to tend to them
as if the powers of the earth
felt the depth of my well
and sent you to fill it

hearts are flowers
when watered correctly
when given enough sun
when planted just right
they bloom
and reveal their colors
but
when they are stepped on
when they drown
when they are left unattended
they wilt
and die
i let you in my garden
expecting you to
love me correctly
want me enough
kiss me just right
you did not
you stepped on the flower
you drowned the flower
and you left it here to wilt
all of my petals fell off
when you left me
for another flower

at a certain point
the poems about you must stop
the deep loneliness must stop
the fantasizing about you must stop
with that
i must conclude
the *chapter of you*

i tasted dinner on your lips
i felt the tension in your hips
i eased your body with a kiss

drowning in a sea
of uncertainty
always left wondering
does he really want me

you make
the earth shake
the oceans move
the sky change
my body nervous
you control it all

your love is a wasp’s sting
there is something oddly peculiar
about enjoying the pain
but i want you to sting me again

fireworks go off in my mind
when i think of you and me

your body is a jungle
let me explore the dangers within

bonfires pale in comparison
to how brightly our love shines
the sun is envious of our rays
the moon cowers at our darkside
the wind wishes to have the power we do
the sea desires to move as rapidly as us
our love supersedes the powers of nature

put you in my mouth
thinking you were sweet
had to spit you out
you were too sour

in the era of contempt
we found each other
and you sheltered me
from the war raging outside

beware the man who says
i do not think i deserve you
his ego is raging
as he waits for you
to validate him
he seeks to be empowered
it makes your pain
more pleasurable
to him

i do not know which is worse
the fact that you left me
or that i was naïve enough
to believe you would stay

a beautiful symphony we were
the medley moved minds
the chords melted hearts
the bridge mended souls
then you hit the wrong note
and the crowd became angry
the flowers they threw
turned into sharp objects
as they booed you off the stage
and i admit
i joined them
you ruined the showcase

warning

caution tape
should have been wrapped around you
should have lined the path that led to you
you are a hazard
and i wish i had been warned

i love you, but i love me more

time is too precious to waste
crying over a boy we both know
was not as pretty as you

with each heartbreak
comes a new wall
around the heart
with each hurt endured
comes intensified trust issues
you want to fall in love
but your heart remembers
the pain you suffered
when your last love left
so you hide behind the walls
and starve yourself of intimacy
because with each heartbreak
comes a deeper fear of love

chaotically
hypnotically
erotically
chronically
obsessed with you

i would give up
all of my remaining minutes with others
for one more minute with you

waiting anxiously
to meet the boy
who shows me
why you were not
supposed to be
my boy

text tones

checking my phone
for a text from you
hoping your name will appear
when i hit the power button
wishing to see
those six letters
when the screen lights up
my stomach drops
every time the phone rings
i am craving words from you
even if the words cut deep wounds
at least the words
will have come from you

unrequited love
is the movie that
plays in my theatre
always
i find myself attached
willing
ready
only to feel them pull away
and reject

i fight so hard
to make them stay
and it only pushes them
further
i attempt to turn
unrequited
into something romantic
it makes the pain tolerable
it makes the rejection bearable

it was only when i convinced myself
that you would stay and love me
that you decided to leave me
maybe i should stop convincing myself
that these boys will actually stick around
that these boys really do want me

how quickly we went
from allies
to adversaries
from falling in loving
to feeling like foes
if the falling
turned to loathing
so quickly
were we ever in love
or just refusing to leave
were we good for each other
or just scared to be alone
if the falling
turned to abhorring
so swiftly
how real was the love
if there was even any at all
we went from fighting for each other
to fighting each other
was it even real love
or was it just self hatred

your cage
i mistook for safety
your lies
i mistook for romance
your abuse
i mistook for love

chemically
it started
ephemerally
it went
lethally
it ended

you told me that i wasn’t a fling
but you left me
before winter became spring

fate can bring two people together
just as quickly as *fear* can tear them apart

daydreams of you
distract me
dreams of you
keep me awake

the words
they were on the tip of your tongue
why didn't you say them
those three words are lethal
they carry power
but those three words
could have saved us
you almost said them
i saw it in your eyes
as i sat on top of you
i was ready to hear them
they would have saved us
maybe that's why you didn't say them
did you not want us to be saved
did you want me to leave
was i kidding myself
was i the only one
in love

tried showering you off my body
with tears of blood
they streamed down my face
they covered me
the way you used to cover me
i am soaked in them
the shirt that i wore that night
is soaked in them
like a wine stain on white sheets
these tears are leaving stains on my heart
bloody tears
after you left
i cried
bloody tears

seeing him with you
leaves me scathing
i would kill him
if given the chance
the way his hands touch you
the way his lips kiss you
the way his words fill you
you and i know
it will never compare
to how i made you feel

the landscape of love
you and i once walked on
has become a battlefield
our armies stand ready
preparing for the war
we once fought together

loved the body
betrayed the heart
maybe you wanted a tinman
someone to kiss
but not enough to love
someone to fuck with
but not enough to miss
someone to flirt with
but not enough to want
luckily
my heart forgives you
my brain learns from pain
my courage keeps me going
you can continue to be
as cruel as you want
drag me and diss me
throw my name in the mud
i'll stay silent
while you turn green and
envy the way i can move on
loath how deeply i can love
despise the strength i have
you're just so hotheaded
i'm surprised that you haven't
already melted from the heat
i'll throw a bucket of tears on you
and watch you seep into the cracks
of the broken promises you made

maybe you didn't mean to lead me on
maybe you didn't mean to hurt me
maybe you didn't mean to break my heart
but you did
i can convince myself that i knew you
that your intentions were to love me
but you just didn't know how to
or maybe you were too scared to
i can convince myself that you didn't hurt me
but you did

i envy the bed you sleep on
i want to be under you like that

your fingers traced my lips
like a map leading you home

ink stains of heartbreak
saturate the parchment
this was my story
this was my memoir
until you spilled heartbreak's ink
and left me here to clean it
the words i had written
were covered in black liquid
leaving me scrambling to remember
what was underneath the ink
what came before the pain of you
all that's left is what you did
and i'm watching it bleed through
all of my pages
ruining each of them
destroying the blank sheets
i had saved for future loves
when i write new stories
the pain you caused
will still be visible
the pain you caused
has stained my story

i remember that phone call
when you promised to protect me
when you said you'd never hurt me
when you said that you were falling for me
i also remember the text that you sent
when you said you were leaving
when the pain cut me deep
when you started falling away
those memories are indelible in the heart

i was ready for a love
that would last until
tomorrow
and then forevermore
but you were stuck in
yesterday

you checked out my heart
with an expired card
and when you decided
you didn’t like my story
you threw it away
and never returned it

games are fun
we played them together
i didn't know
that i was a game
to you

when others play *the album of us*
will they fall in love with our songs
will the tracks spark romance
will the imagery light up the night

i spent so many nights
crying in my bed
hoping my river of tears
would bring your ship back
but my port is still empty
a flood of tears surrounds me
and you are nowhere to be found

i just met you and already
you’re healing my past
you’re consuming my present
you’re all i want for my future
time is fickle and precious
and i want to give you
every second i have left to give

fuck the wise men
i’m rushing in

every word you spoke
was like poetry
the way you used your tongue
it puts whitman to shame
it makes simmonds regret
it causes dickinson to quiver
each syllable so clear
each noun spoken with passion
each prose so lively
that tongue
i wonder what else
that tongue can do

how many nights
can i spend in bed
giving my body
through a screen
to men
these men who don’t know me
who don’t even want to
they tell me i’m pretty
but they don’t even know
that every time i hit send
my self worth dies again
when will self love
be something i love
will i always be looking
for a man to validate me
that send button hurts me
it’s like a gunshot in my body
everytime i hit it
knowing he is seeing it
knowing what he’s doing with it
knowing that he’s loving himself
but not here loving me

shattered glass on cobblestone
that's how you left my heart
a million pieces scattered
broke me into so many parts
glass cannot be put back together
it cannot be made to look new
it can be glued together
but the damage was clearly done
each crack peaks through
every shard remains sharp

i get you
is what you said
you understood me
totally accepted
completely as myself
then you left
left me blindsided
my *i get you, too*
has become
he left me too

you gave me
your last summer here
i gave you my heart
i gave you my body
words fail me
i cannot describe
how grateful i am
for the love that we shared
it taught me to grow
it made me feel deeply
it showed me real safety
words fail me
i am in love with you

why can’t i stop
thinking about you

someone new
is laying here
right next to me
but i’m only thinking
he is where you
ought to be

i kiss him
but not like i kissed you
i hold him
but not as tightly as i held you
i miss him
but not as painfully as i missed you

have you ever loved someone
that was never yours to love
nothing holds back a heart
like a one-way love
you find it easy to miss them
when you barely touched them

but then it is impossible to love the one
you have on your skin
at this moment
because your heart is still holding out
for that love that left
before the love began

i’m still in my driveway
waiting for your truck
to come back
to pick me up
to take me back
to that night we shared
in january

dangerous waters

i view my life
as an ocean storm
waves are crashing
tides are raging
winds are thrashing
dangerous to swim
impossible to survive

then one day
you threw a life raft
it had your name it on
it guided me home
brought me to your shore
i felt the warmth
i felt the safety
i felt the calm

dangerous waters *(continued)*

suddenly you left
and i was pushed back to sea
but i was still in your life raft
and now i can't get out
your name is on the mast
your protection is found inside
it keeps me above the waves

without you
i'm lost at sea
with you
i'm lost in love
i still have your life raft
just come back
come sail it with me

i’ve never felt pain so intensely
if only he were here to ease it
but what he doesn’t know is that
i would endure more pain
if i could just see him again
just to kiss his lips again

there is nothing in this world
that i wouldn’t give
to see his face again
no amount of pain i wouldn’t pay
no amount of heartache i wouldn’t endure
just to see him once more

more than once this month
i’ve gone to my window
and sat down beside it
looking and waiting
for your car to pull up
hoping you’ll come back
and tell me you love me
it may be wrong and unfair
but what’s more unfair
is that you aren’t mine

part two:

family, self, & others

cut me when i was weak
mocked how i was meek
the cut you left still leaks

gaslighting

i'm sorry you feel that way
is a bad excuse
i'm sorry you feel that way
is just a clever way of saying
don't be triggered by my abuse

from you
father
i inherited
wounds
sores
pain
anger
scars

sundays were for prayers
mondays were for pain

family cycle

hate is hereditary
it is not taught
it is passed down

i write my own story

i will not be defined
by the crimes of my father
by the decisions of my mother
by the prayers of my grandfather
i will create my own course

home was hell

a son of adam
locked out of eden
the abuse he endured
at the hands of his father
locked him in
a personal hell

6610 Rockwood Dr.

nothing holds more trauma
than a childhood home

forget your wishes, i want nothing to do with you

you wanted a son
more masculine than myself
one who would throw the ball
chase the girl
hunt and fish wild animals
but instead
you were given me
and rather than nurturing the qualities
you didn't want in me
you made a mockery of them

apple doesn't fall far
oh how wrong that is
i will fall
and fall
and fall
until i can fall no more
and even still
i will find a way to keep falling
as far away from your tree
as i can possibly be
because i would rather be
a broken apple
than an apple
that resembles your tree

your dreams
of me with a wife
of me passing down your name
of me raising a son in your vein
were all shattered
when i brought a man into your home

the only thing
we have in common
is blood
and if i could
i would empty it
from my body

i am nothing like you

you taught me many things
the only thing worth noting
is that i should strive
to do everything
exactly how you
wouldn't

if you are what they call *a real man*
count me out of masculinity

i cannot remember
the last time i experienced peace
calm
still
the voice in my head has killed it
it is never quiet
i cannot escape it
i cannot escape my mind
it is with me forever
these thoughts will be with me forever
it feels like i am constantly being chased
by *wasps that are ready to sting*
but the wasps are already inside my head
they are already stinging
and there is nowhere to flee
because *their nest*
is my mind

anxiety

you are intrusive
and abusive
and oppressive
you are persistent
and dramatic
and petulant
you live in me
you are the jailer
you are the withholder
you are the judge and the victim

fake friends

i could handle the sting
when one of you played me
but i don't know how to handle
you teaming up against me

depression

conversations continue
my mind spins
my body checks out

for the bible told you so

unnatural is the word
you use to describe me
but what is unnatural
about sex
companionship
and love
i am beginning to think
the beliefs you hold
are the only unnatural thing

prosecutor or predator? you decide

your cold eyes
your needy body
your lack of self control
the way you used me
the way you treated me
the way you abused the law
i was a child
and you were an animal
like one in the wild
who needs taming
prepare for the defaming
because
it is in prison
you will be remaining

you taught me how
to identify the predator
you showed me how
to turn in the predator
you told me how
old predators worked
and prepared
and groomed
but *you were the predator*
that loomed

the document that saved me

the divorce decree
was the key
to ending
what was never
meant to be
and though the children
could not see
the marriage
was drowning in a sea
and it was poisoning
the family tree

violated
but survivor
depleted
but survivor
damaged
but survivor

do not mistake my forgiveness
as excusing your behavior

i forgave you
for me

so i could move forward
not so you could feel better

i forgave you
for me

so i could learn to feel strong again
not so you could feel worthy

my forgiveness
demonstrates my strength

your need for my forgiveness
demonstrates your weakness

chains of shame
tell me i am to blame
for trying to end
your cruel game
but the chains will tighten
if i choose to remain

a broken home
is better than broken bones
is better than broken souls
is better than broken minds

this home
needed to be broken
to be safe

prozac numbs
zoloft intensifies
lexapro sedates
co-dependent
on medication
i know them
like the back of my hand
i see them more
than i see my friends
two tablets
twice daily
increase the dose
three times a year
hope my body
does not build tolerance
wishing for the meds
to balance the imbalance
the chemical imbalance
throws my body off balance
slave to sleep
no motivation
waiting for the day
the meds actually help
so i can stop just telling myself
that i am okay
and i can actually
genuinely
feel okay

trauma
is a tattoo
it comes in different shapes
some take longer to heal
others are larger
but they are forever with you
as though the universe
is branding you
is reminding you
of what you went through

the steeple of the church
reminds me of trauma
they preach of heaven
their pews are hell

still precious

i learned to hate myself
at such a young age
the religion of my family
told me i was wrong
said there was something
wrong with me

self hatred grew
and drowned me in a sea
of loathing
i was drowning and burning
all at the same time
self loathing filled my lungs
made it hard to breathe

the words of the churches
burned my skin
left scars there forever
to remind me that i
as myself
loving as i do
am not good enough for them

still precious *(continued)*

that i endanger the children
they view as precious
avoiding the fact that i too
was a child
they once called precious

their love was conditional
as was their god's love
they wanted me in box
and hated me for stepping out

they shield their children
from my path
treat me as parasite
worthy of little love
deserving of hell fire
in need of prayer
the love they preach
ceased
when it was a man
i began to seek

body image

fear of the mirror
haunts each day
i'm afraid to look
as if i think a monster
will be looking back
i hate my reflection

insecurity is throned
in every part of my mind
i fear what others will say
about the way i look
i know nothing of them
but assume they know enough of me
to judge my every move
the mirror horrifies me
why am i so afraid of seeing
my flaws
my imperfections
my scars
i am afraid to see
me

my mind has me convinced
that the mirror decides
if i'm worthy of love
my mind has me convinced
that the mirror decides
if people will love me
why am i so afraid of the mirror
why am i so afraid of me
the way i treat myself
the way i bully who i am
the way i hate what i see

i am the judge
and every day
i find myself guilty
guilty of looking like that
hiding my face
from others
but i can't hide my face
from myself
my reflection
on the wall
i hate you
most of all

in this race of life
you can only go
as far as you’re
willing to run
run at a pace you set
but never stop running
so much lies before you
on the track ahead

puzzle pieces

each piece of my puzzle
is important to me
they make me complete
they allow me to be

you cannot choose
which pieces to use
you must accept
every piece that you see

some pieces are bruised
others shine bright
some pieces are scarred
others are just alright

but each piece of my puzzle
is important to me
each piece of my puzzle
is needed to see

needed to see
the person i know i can be
each puzzle piece is needed
to see me

mortal

innocence marked year *one*
blue eyes full of life and hope
two came around like a rainstorm
tantrums and games and naps
three hit like a freight train
so much energy and a voice to speak
four witnessed the beginning of difference
a predisposition to be uncovered
by *five* my little hands could write the words
the words that filled my supple mind
at *six* the dawns broke early
breakfast was prepared as the bus pulled up
when the clock struck midnight at the age of *seven*
that predisposition had been awoken
eight years old and craving knowledge
such a loud voice for such a small creature
nine endured the trauma of confusion
the experiences of the body rattled the mind
ten had much to offer my soul
much growth and change occurred

mortal (*continued)*

eleven saw the downfall of sanity
abuse was now seen for what it really was
twelve began the markings on the body
left by the hands i called my own
thirteen found solace in the friends of life
but some were only pretending
fourteen felt the growth of the body
development became so painfully awkward
fifteen spurred exploration of others
in mind and body both
sixteen was the age of much pain
the body was confused once again
seventeen is the age of too much regret
of wishing i hadn't grown so fast
eighteen feels like an infinity away
so far in the distance yet right here today
each year that passes
each wrinkle that comes
each breath that exists
reminds me that i am
mortal

afterword

though i am unsure of who said it first,
make your mess your message
is a phrase i live by.
and these poems were written with that phrase in mind.
the idea that humans hold the ability to shape their future,
shift the narrative,
and shut out the negative voices brings me hope.
for my future and the future of others.
my life is my mess.
the abuse i endured at the hands of
evangelicals, family, and adults in my circle…
it all culminates to my mess.
but rather than sitting by and allowing their wrongdoings
to ruin the future i desired for myself,
i made the mess my message.
take your mess, make it your message.

- carter zane

a final note for the reader...

remember: while each of these poems is intensely focused,
they reflect my own point of view.
each person that prompted the poems
will certainly view each situation differently than i did.

i hope you have enjoyed reading these poems
as much as i enjoyed writing them.

affectionately,

c.z.

about the author

carter zane was born in east texas.
he moved to the dallas, tx area when he was 15.
he has a passion for equality and lgbtqia+ youth rights.
carter can often be found taking long walks,
reading a stephen king novel,
drinking an unhealthy amount of coffee,
binge watching *gilmore girls*,
and shuffle playing *speak now* by taylor swift.
carter has plans to go into the legal field.

you can find him on instagram:

@ carterzanee

www.ingramcontent.com/pod-product-compliance
Ingram Content Group UK Ltd.
Pitfield, Milton Keynes, MK11 3LW, UK
UKHW041845200726
13854UKWH00005BA/2146

9 798518 527546